BAR MITZVAH

by HOWARD GREENFELD
illustrated by ELAINE GROVE

Holt, Rinehart and Winston • New York

Text copyright © 1981 by Howard Greenfeld
Illustrations copyright © 1981 by Elaine Grove
All rights reserved, including the right to reproduce
this book or portions thereof in any form.
Published simultaneously in Canada by Holt, Rinehart
and Winston of Canada, Limited.
Printed in the United States of America
10   9   8   7   6   5   4   3   2   1

Library of Congress Cataloging in Publication Data

Greenfeld, Howard.
Bar mitzvah.

Summary: Describes the origins and significance
of the bar mitzvah and the ceremony attached to it.
Also highlights the bat mitzvah.
1. Bar mitzvah—Juvenile literature. [1. Bar mitzvah.
2. Jews—Rites and ceremonies] I. Grove, Elaine.
II. Title
BM707.G73   296.4'424   81-5104
ISBN 0-03-053861-0   AACR2

BAR MITZVAH

The celebration of the *bar mitzvah* is today one of the most significant occasions in the life of a Jew. The words themselves mean "son of the commandment," and upon becoming bar mitzvah a young Jew becomes subject to and responsible for obedience to the divine commandments or laws that govern the lives of all Jews. It signifies the end of his childhood and the beginning of the period of young manhood and maturity, the time when he assumes a new role in the Jewish community.

The day of the bar mitzvah ceremony is a very special one. It is a day of solemnity, since the occasion marks the acceptance by the boy of new privileges and responsibilities. It is also a day of happiness for him and for his family, as well as for the entire congregation as they gather to witness the ceremony of a new member joining their ranks.

Above all, it is a day of celebration for the boy. This is his own day. He is the newest member of the community and the center of attention. Feelings of importance mingle with a certain embarrassment over the amount of attention and love he receives and with some nervousness as he is called upon for the first time to perform his duties as a Jew.

The formal religious ceremony marking this unique occasion usually, but not always, takes place in the synagogue. Following the ceremony, it has become customary to celebrate with a party for the boy's family and friends. It is a time of great joy and sometimes even of extravagance, a fitting climax to this memorable day. Nonetheless, the celebration must not obscure the real meaning of this turning point in the life of a Jew. For this reason, it is important to learn of the origins of the bar mitzvah, its full significance, and the ceremony attached to it.

No two people mature at the same time or at the same rate. Nor do any of us reach the age at which we can assume responsibility for our own acts at any single given moment. To reach maturity is a slow, gradual process, making it impossible to say that one day a person is a child and on the next he or she becomes an adult. In spite of this, certain fixed dates in our lives have come to be considered important as turning points along the road from childhood to maturity.

According to the Bible we are not ready to assume full civic responsibilities as adults until our twentieth year. For example, it is written in the Book of Numbers that the

Lord asked Moses to list the names of all males from the age of twenty years and up, so that they might be called to bear arms. This establishes a biblical law.

Nations too have laws. According to those laws, which are subject to change, we reach maturity at some time between the ages of eighteen and twenty-one. At that time, we begin to enjoy full rights, such as the right to vote. We also take on full responsibilities of citizenship — among them that of defending our country in time of danger.

These civic laws, which are written down, regulate our society at large.

In the Jewish faith, there are both written laws and laws based on tradition.

The bar mitzvah is not a written law. It is a "law" that has grown out of tradition. A Jew attains religious maturity when he enters his fourteenth year (that is, one day after his thirteenth birthday). At that time, he becomes bar mitzvah. This means that he takes responsibilities for obeying the commandments of the written law.

There is no complete agreement among scholars as to the precise origin of this belief that a Jew is ready to assume his duties as a Jew following his thirteenth birthday. But the age of thirteen has long been a signifi-

cant one for every male Jew. This is noted in two fundamental books of Jewish knowledge and wisdom, the *Midrash* and the *Talmud*.

The *Midrash* is a collection of early rabbinic commentaries, written down between the second and eleventh centuries, based on a minute examination and interpretation of the Bible. From it we learn that it was at the age of thirteen that Abraham destroyed his father's idols and became the first Jew. It was at thirteen, too, that Jacob and Esau, the twin sons of Isaac, son of Abraham, separated, with Jacob following the ways of the Torah while his brother set out to worship idols.

More specific mention of the important change in the young Jew's position in the community is found in the *Talmud*. This work is second in importance to the Bible as a foundation of Judaism. It is a massive compilation of and commentary upon not the Bible but Jewish oral law. Touching on every aspect of human life and compiled over a period of five centuries, it contains more than three million words, and is divided into two parts: the *Mishnah*, which sets down the texts of these unwritten laws; and the *Gemara*, which discusses and comments upon them. It is written in the Tal-

mud that boys begin to develop into men following their thirteenth birthday. Until that time it is a father's responsibility to raise his son; after that, it is the boy himself who must be called to account for his own acts. Clearly, the father continues to be responsible for many aspects of the boy's life — including his education — following his thirteenth birthday. But at the ceremony celebrating the bar mitzvah the father is able to recite a special benediction recognizing a change in his son's status.

Further mention of the coming of age of a young Jew is found in the *Pirke Avot*, a section in the Mishnah. It contains sayings of the wise men from the third century B.C.E. (Before the Common Era) to the third century C.E. (Common Era). This work says that at the age of thirteen a child is brought to the commandments; that is, after this time it is his duty to perform the religious practices which apply to all adult male Jews.

Among these practices are all those associated with Jewish religious holidays such as the day-long fast on Yom Kippur, the Day of Atonement, and the spending of that entire day in the synagogue among the adults instead of attending special children's services which are now held in many

synagogues. Just as many obligations are assumed, many formal privileges are granted. Among the privileges, for the first time a young Jew can be called up before the congregation to participate in the reading from the *Torah*, which is also known as the Scroll of the Law. In addition, on becoming bar mitzvah, a young Jew can be accepted as a member of the quorum of ten adult males necessary, under Jewish law, for the recital of communal prayers. This quorum is known as a *minyan*. It symbolizes the communal nature of the Jewish religion. No wedding service or *Kaddish* — mourner's prayer — is legally valid without the presence of a minimum of ten males of at least bar mitzvah age. They may gather together for the purpose of prayer, with or without a rabbi, in or outside of a synagogue.

Among the boy's new obligations is that of wearing a *tallit* during his morning prayers (and all day on Yom Kippur). This special fringed prayer shawl, square in shape, is made of white cloth, usually silk or wool. Woven in the cloth are blue (or sometimes black) stripes, in fulfillment of a biblical commandment found in the Book of Numbers. These colors are of significance: the white stands for purity of

thought, while the blue is a reminder that one's thoughts must go skyward, toward heaven (if black is used, it is as a reminder of the fall of the Temple).

Another obligation asssumed upon reaching the age of bar mitzvah is that of putting on the *tefillin*: this word has the same root as the Hebrew word for prayer — *tefilla*. The *tefillin* are two small black leather boxes containing four pieces of parchment. Written on the parchment are four passages from the Books of Exodus and Deuteronomy. These verses from the Scriptures affirm the Jew's allegiance to and love for God and pledge obedience to the divine commandments. They urge the Jewish people to love their God with all their heart, with all their soul, and with all their might.

Attached to these cubical boxes are two leather straps. One binds the box to the man's forehead (close to his brain and therefore his thoughts) and one to his left arm (close to his heart). These are intended as a reminder of man's bond to God and are worn each morning during prayer. According to the Talmud, when a boy comes of age, his father presents him with tefillin, instructing him in their use and care.

These practices are symbolic of the

young Jew's new position as a full member of the community, and the obligation to perform specific rituals. These vary among the three movements of Judaism — the Orthodox, Conservative, and Reform. All three adhere to the fundamental beliefs of the Jewish religion, but their ways of observing their faith differ in several areas. Orthodox Jews believe that the law handed down to Moses is unalterable, that the Bible and Talmud are absolute authorities, down to the smallest detail. Conservative Jews hold to this tradition for the most part, but they differ in believing that some gradual, moderate changes in observance are permissible in accordance with changes which have taken place in society. Reform Jews, too, adhere to the doctrines, but they believe that the observances and rituals of Judaism must change with the times, reflecting the social and cultural needs and customs of each succeeding generation.

To cite but one difference, in an Orthodox synagogue, all prayers are recited in Hebrew. In a Conservative synagogue, the prayers are largely recited in Hebrew. In a Reform synagogue, they are generally recited in the everyday language of the people. So it is too that the rights and obligations of a bar mitzvah

differ according to the movement to which the parents of the boy belong. For example, the Reform Jew does not don the tefillin, nor is he required to wear the tallit while praying as is the case with the Orthodox and Conservative. These are not symbols of a Reform Jew's coming of age.

The actual ceremony celebrating the bar mitzvah differs among the three movements of Judaism, according to the rituals each observes. In addition, it has varied from one period of time to another and from one country to another. A principal cause for these variations lies in the fact that the ceremony marking bar mitzvah is of relatively recent origin, and thus there is no long tradition to be followed. In fact, the first specific directions for this ritual are not found until the sixteenth century. They appear in the *Shulchan Aruch* (the Prepared Table), a minutely detailed guide to Jewish law, written by Joseph Caro. Though there are mentions of some kind of ritual celebrating this event as early as the sixth century, the bar mitzvah was, most often, considered an automatic achievement, not marked by any special observance or celebration. It was commonly assumed that by his thirteenth birthday a Jewish boy had

SHULCHAN ARUCH
• • •
THE
PRE-
PARED
TABLE

JOSEPH CARO

REPARED
TABLE
THE PREPARED
TABLE

had sufficient religious training in and out of the home to enable him to qualify as a full member of the Jewish community, and no festivities were needed to signal this change in his status.

With time, however, an adequate Jewish education for each young boy could no longer be taken for granted. As the demands and distractions of society increased, and the importance of nonsectarian public education grew, the religious education of the young Jew was often neglected. Because of this, the achievement of bar mitzvah became something special. Today as many as four years of careful preparation might be required before a boy is deemed ready to participate in what is a kind of graduation ceremony. It marks the end of one stage of his religious training. The training consists of studies in the Hebrew language and literature, in the history of the Jewish people, and courses which lead to an understanding of Jewish law and tradition. For this purpose, many synagogues hold special classes to prepare a boy for bar mitzvah so that by the age of thirteen he will be ready to take his place as a member of the community.

The eagerly anticipated bar mitzvah ceremony is generally a part of the regular

Saturday morning services, held on the first Sabbath following the boy's thirteenth birthday. In the course of this service, the boy — often accompanied by his father and other members of his family — is for the first time called up before the congregation to take his place on the *bimah*, the pulpit, which is in front of the synagogue. On this bimah stands the desk on which the Torah is opened and then read.

The boy begins his solemn task by reciting a *beraca*, or blessing, over the Torah. It is read, portion by portion, throughout the year. In this blessing, he praises the Lord who has chosen the Jews from among all people and given them His Law. Immediately afterward, he recites either one *parsha* (portion) or the entire weekly *sidra* (lesson) from the Torah. This reading is the essential part of the ceremony, the culmination of his studies; it confirms his new status as a bar mitzvah.

Following this, he pronounces another blessing. This time he praises the Lord for revealing the law of truth and righteousness to the Jewish people, after which he reads a portion from the words of the Prophets. This portion is called *Haftarah*, the Hebrew word for "conclusion."

After the boy has finished his readings,

his father is called upon to recite his own blessing appropriate to that day. He affirms his gratitude to God that his son has reached the age of responsibility, declaring: "Blessed be Thou our God who has relieved me of the responsibility for this child."

The Sabbath morning service, conducted by the rabbi, continues. In the course of it, other members of the family might be called upon to participate. Often the boy himself is asked to deliver a speech in which he expresses his gratitude to his parents, affirms his dedication to the ideals of Judaism, or demonstrates the fruits of his training by making a scholarly discourse on some aspect of Talmudic law.

Finally, there is usually a special sermon by the rabbi, addressed for the most part to the boy, reminding him of his new duties as well as his new privileges as a full member of the congregation, and blessing him. This is the conclusion of the formal religious ceremony.

Now the young man, having performed his new responsibilities as a Jew, can relax and enjoy the less formal activities that are also a part of this bar mitzvah celebration. This is the party, a joyous one to which friends and family are invited to share in the happiness of the young man. There are

gifts, and possibly a few speeches — lighthearted ones — and, inevitably, there is a banquet fit for this special occasion. No ordinary party, it has roots in a Jewish tradition dating from the Middle Ages. It is called a *seudat mitzvah*, a festive meal in celebration of a special occasion in the life of a Jew, such as a circumcision, a wedding, or a bar mitzvah.

As contemporary Jews increasingly seek to assert their identity as Jews, the bar mitzvah ceremony grows yearly in importance, and has been adjusted to modern social conditions. Since there is no religious decree establishing the age at which the ceremony must be performed, Jews of all ages, who had failed to perform the ritual at the age of thirteen, are performing it whenever they feel a need to strengthen their bonds with the Jewish community. Thus, it is no longer unusual to find a man of thirty or forty or fifty — sometimes older — formally celebrating his bar mitzvah for the first time. He may automatically become bar mitzvah on his thirteenth birthday, but he is free to celebrate and affirm this fact at any time.

The setting for the bar mitzvah ceremony, too, has not been prescribed by law,

and it can vary widely. Often it takes place far from a synagogue. Some Jews travel to distant places, such as the holy Western Wall of Jerusalem, for this rite. It was recently reported that two inmates — well over the usual bar mitzvah age — celebrated their coming of age as Jews within the walls of a Texas prison.

The most significant modern development has been the introduction of the *bat mitzvah* ceremony. Bat mitzvah means "daughter of the commandment," and the ceremony celebrates a girl's coming of age. Its frequency has grown as the important role of women in society has been recognized. Along with their fight for social, cultural, and economic equality with men, Jewish women have demanded and are attaining religious equality; there are today women rabbis among Reform congregations.

The bat mitzvah ceremony differs in some respects from that which celebrates the bar mitzvah. It usually takes place on the girl's twelfth birthday, a recognition of the fact that girls mature at an earlier age than do boys. Frequently, the girl does not read from the Torah scroll itself, but instead recites certain given prayers as well as a portion from the Haftarah. The bat

mitzvah ceremony is performed among Reform and Conservative congregations, but it is not recognized by Orthodox Jews. Jewish women have not yet achieved complete equality with men, but they are no longer thought of as merely mothers and housewives. In celebrating their bat mitzvah, girls can, today, also take their places as full members of the Jewish community.

BAR MITZVAH